I0430194

U.S. ENVIRONMENTAL PROTECTION AGENCY
OFFICE OF INSPECTOR GENERAL

Catalyst for Improving the Environment

Evaluation Report

Key Activities in EPA's Integrated Urban Air Toxics Strategy Remain Unimplemented

Report No. 10-P-0154

June 23, 2010

Report Contributors:

Rick Beusse
Bao Chuong
Erica Hauck
Jim Hatfield
Rebecca Matichuk
Michael Young

Abbreviations

CAA	Clean Air Act
CARE	Community Action for a Renewed Environment
EPA	U.S. Environmental Protection Agency
FY	Fiscal Year
GACT	Generally Available Control Technology
GAO	U.S. Government Accountability Office
HAP	Hazardous Air Pollutant
MACT	Maximum Achievable Control Technology
NACAA	National Association of Clean Air Agencies
NATA	National-Scale Air Toxics Assessment
OAQPS	Office of Air Quality Planning and Standards
OAR	Office of Air and Radiation
OIG	Office of Inspector General
S/L/T	State, local, and tribal

Cover photo: Stationary and mobile sources in Chicago, Illinois. (Photo courtesy of the *Chicago Tribune*, accompanying article titled "Our Toxic Air," September 29, 2008.)

At a Glance

Catalyst for Improving the Environment

Why We Did This Review

The public health risk from exposure to air toxics is a concern in many urban areas. Accordingly, we conducted this evaluation to assess how the U.S. Environmental Protection Agency (EPA) tracks progress toward the goals of its 1999 Integrated Urban Air Toxics Strategy. The Clean Air Act (CAA) Amendments of 1990 required EPA to develop this Strategy to reduce public health risks from air toxics emissions in urban areas.

Background

Air toxics are emitted from a variety of sources, including major sources (refineries, power plants), small stationary sources (dry cleaners, gas stations), and mobile sources (cars, trucks, construction equipment). Excessive exposure to air toxics may result in increased risks of cancer and noncancer diseases affecting the human respiratory, reproductive, and neurological systems.

For further information, contact our Office of Congressional, Public Affairs and Management at (202) 566-2391.

To view the full report, click on the following link: www.epa.gov/oig/reports/2010/20100623-10-P-0154.pdf

Key Activities in EPA's Integrated Urban Air Toxics Strategy Remain Unimplemented

What We Found

EPA has not implemented key requirements of CAA Section 112(k), including developing emission standards for all area (smaller) source categories and submitting a second report to Congress (due in 2002) identifying urban areas that continue to experience significant public health risks from air toxics exposures. In addition, 10 years after issuing the 1999 Integrated Urban Air Toxics Strategy, EPA has still not implemented key activities outlined in the Strategy. For example, EPA has not established baseline risk data to measure progress in reducing air toxics risks. As a result, EPA has not tracked progress in meeting the Strategy's goals.

Further, although EPA determined in 2001 that a risk-based program is necessary to meet the goals of the Strategy, EPA has not yet determined whether it has the statutory authority to require State and local agencies to implement such a program. Many State and local agencies do not have their own risk-based programs, and about half of the States and several local agencies have laws preventing them from implementing environmental regulations stricter than EPA's regulations. Without the establishment of a minimum, federally required risk-based program, we do not believe that all State and local agencies will implement programs to adequately address the health risks from urban air toxics.

EPA's last risk assessment, based on 2002 data, estimated that 1 in every 28,000 people could develop cancer from air toxics exposure, and that 2 million Americans live in areas with lifetime cancer risks from air toxics in excess of 1 in 10,000. Given the length of time since the Integrated Urban Air Toxics Strategy was developed and the problems EPA has encountered in its implementation, EPA should reassess and update its approach to addressing urban air toxics.

What We Recommend

We recommend that EPA (1) submit the required second report to Congress, which should include a list of urban areas that continue to experience high or unacceptable levels of risk and EPA's plan to reduce risks in those areas, as well as the factors that have hindered implementation of the Strategy and EPA's plan to address those factors; and (2) determine how it will measure progress in meeting the goals of the Strategy. EPA partially agreed with our recommendations, but did not agree to include the full list of issues in its second report to Congress, or to inform Congress if it decides to measure progress against a baseline other than a 1990 or similar baseline. EPA said it would reassess its position when submitting its corrective action plan. We consider the recommendations open and unresolved.

UNITED STATES ENVIRONMENTAL PROTECTION AGENCY
WASHINGTON, D.C. 20460

June 23, 2010

MEMORANDUM

SUBJECT: Key Activities in EPA's Integrated Urban Air Toxics Strategy
Remain Unimplemented
Report No. 10-P-0154

FROM: Wade T. Najjum
Assistant Inspector General for Program Evaluation

TO: Gina McCarthy
Assistant Administrator for Air and Radiation

This is our report on the subject evaluation conducted by the Office of Inspector General (OIG) of the U.S. Environmental Protection Agency (EPA). This report contains findings that describe the problems the OIG has identified and corrective actions the OIG recommends. This report represents the opinion of the OIG and does not necessarily represent the final EPA position. Final determinations on matters in this report will be made by EPA managers in accordance with established audit resolution procedures.

The estimated cost of this report – calculated by multiplying the project's staff days by the applicable daily full cost billing rates in effect at the time – is $586,976.

Action Required

In accordance with EPA Manual 2750, you are required to provide a written response to this report within 90 calendar days. You should include a corrective actions plan for agreed-upon actions, including milestone dates. However, as discussed in the report, we do not believe your planned actions meet the full intent of the recommendations and we consider all recommendations to be unresolved. We ask that you review our comments and reconsider your responses. We have no objections to the further release of this report to the public. This report will be available at http://www.epa.gov/oig.

If you or your staff have any questions regarding this report, please contact me at (202) 566-0832 or najjum.wade@epa.gov, or Rick Beusse at (919) 541-5747 or beusse.rick@epa.gov.

Table of Contents

Chapters

Appendices

Chapter 1
Introduction

Purpose

Section 112(k) of the Clean Air Act (CAA) Amendments of 1990 required the U.S. Environmental Protection Agency (EPA) to develop a strategy to reduce public health risks in urban areas from air toxics emissions, particularly from small stationary sources. EPA issued its Integrated Urban Air Toxics Strategy in 1999 to meet this requirement.

Our overall assignment objective was to evaluate the status of EPA, State, and local agency efforts to control urban air toxics. Specifically, we assessed how EPA tracks progress with the three goals of the Strategy, which are to:

- Attain a 75 percent reduction in the incidence of cancer attributable to exposure to hazardous air pollutants (HAPs)[1] emitted by large and small stationary sources nationwide.

- Attain a substantial reduction in public health risks (such as birth defects and reproduction effects) posed by HAP emissions from small industrial/commercial sources known as area sources.

- Address disproportionate impacts of air toxics hazards across urban areas, such as geographic "hot spots," highly exposed population subgroups, and predominately minority and low-income communities.

Background

EPA defines air toxics as those pollutants that are known or suspected to cause cancer or other serious health effects or adverse environmental effects. EPA regulates 187 air toxics under the CAA. Over half of these pollutants are known or suspected to cause cancer. In addition, many air toxics cause noncancer effects such as damage to the immune, respiratory, neurological, reproductive, and developmental systems, particularly in susceptible populations such as children. Individuals exposed to air toxics at sufficient concentrations and durations may have an increased chance of developing cancer or experiencing other serious health effects.

---

[1] The CAA uses the term hazardous air pollutants or HAPs. EPA also refers to HAPs as air toxics. Throughout this report, we use the term air toxics to describe the 187 HAPs identified by the CAA.

Air toxics are emitted from a wide variety of sources, including stationary sources, mobile sources, and natural sources like forest fires. Stationary sources include both major and area sources. Major sources are large facilities like petroleum refineries, factories, and power plants. Area sources are smaller facilities and include dry cleaners, gas stations, and auto body repair shops. Mobile sources consist of on-road sources, such as cars and trucks, as well as non-road sources, such as construction equipment, marine vessels, and lawn and garden equipment. Table 1-1 provides more information on the sources of air toxics emissions.

Table 1-1: Sources of Air Toxics

Source	Definition	Examples
Stationary:		
Major	Emissions of 10 tons per year or more of any one air toxic, or 25 tons per year or more of any combination of air toxics	Utilities, refineries, steel manufacturers, chemical manufacturers
Area	Emissions of less than 10 tons per year of any one air toxic pollutant, or less than 25 tons per year of any combination of air toxics	Dry cleaners, gas stations, auto body refinishing paint shops, decorative chromium electroplating operations
Mobile:		
On-road	Emissions from motorized vehicles normally operated on public roadways	Cars, buses, sport-utility vehicles, light- and heavy-duty trucks
Non-road	Emissions from a diverse collection of engines, equipment, vehicles, and vessels operated off public roads	Construction and agricultural equipment, personal watercraft, lawn and garden equipment

Source: OIG.

Air toxics emissions in urban areas can be of particular concern because of the large number and variety of sources, the high concentration of these sources in urban areas, and the large number of people – including sensitive subpopulations such as children and the elderly – exposed to emissions. EPA periodically provides quantitative estimates of cancer and noncancer risks from air toxics through its National-Scale Air Toxics Assessments (NATAs). EPA's latest assessment (based on 2002 emissions data) estimated that 2 million Americans lived in areas where the increased lifetime risk from air toxics exposure was greater than 1 in 10,000. Appendix A describes in more detail EPA's estimates of cancer risk and the potential for adverse noncancer health effects from air toxics exposure based on 2002 air toxics emissions.

Federal Requirements to Reduce Air Toxics Emissions and Risks

Prior to 1990, the CAA established a risk-based air toxics program under which only a few emission standards were developed. To address the lack of progress and the difficulty in setting standards based on risk, the CAA Amendments of 1990 established a two-phase approach for addressing air toxics emissions from stationary sources. First, the CAA Amendments required EPA to issue technology-based standards for certain categories, or industry groupings, of major and area sources. In the second phase, EPA is required to implement a risk-based program to ensure the protection of public health and the environment. These two phases are discussed in more detail below.

Technology-Based Phase Includes MACT and GACT Standards

For major source categories, the CAA required EPA to establish emission standards that reflect the maximum degree of reductions in emissions of air toxics achieved by sources in that industry. These emission standards are commonly referred to as maximum achievable control technology (MACT) standards, and must reflect, at a minimum, the level of emission control achieved by the top 12 percent of performers in the industry. EPA has issued MACT standards for all of the major source categories. In total, EPA issued 96 MACT standards from 1993 to 2004, covering 174 different source categories.

The CAA allows EPA to develop standards for area sources that are less stringent than those for major sources. If EPA deems it appropriate, it can set standards for area source categories based on generally available control technology (GACT) rather than MACT. GACT is defined as "methods, practices, and techniques which are commercially available and appropriate for application by the sources in the category considering economic impacts and the technical capabilities of the firms to operate and maintain the emissions control systems." As of January 2010, EPA had issued standards for 66 of the 70 area source categories.

Risk-Based Phase Includes Residual Risk Rules and the Integrated Urban Air Toxics Strategy

In the second phase of the air toxics program, the CAA requires EPA to meet certain risk-based goals for public health. Eight years after the technology-based MACT standards are issued for a source category, EPA is required to review those standards to determine whether any residual risk exists for that source category. If necessary, EPA must revise the standard to protect public health with "an ample margin of safety." To provide an ample margin of safety, EPA strives to limit the risk of cancer for the most people to no greater than 1 in 1 million, and limit the risk to the most exposed individual to no greater than 1 in 10,000. Area sources regulated by a GACT standard are not subject to this residual risk requirement. As of January 2010, EPA had finalized residual risk rules for 20 of the 174 MACT source categories, and proposed rules for an additional 9 source categories.

The risk-based phase of the federal air toxics program also includes the Integrated Urban Air Toxics Strategy. CAA Section 112(k) requires EPA to develop a comprehensive strategy to control emissions from area sources in urban areas and reduce public health risks from all stationary sources. Specifically, Section 112(k)(3)(c) requires EPA to include in its strategy:

> . . . a schedule of specific actions to substantially reduce the public health risks posed by the release of hazardous air pollutants from area sources . . . The strategy shall achieve a reduction in the incidence of cancer attributable to exposure to hazardous air pollutants emitted by stationary sources of not less than 75 per centum . . .

EPA finalized the Integrated Urban Air Toxics Strategy in 1999 to meet this requirement. Although the CAA requirement focused on stationary sources, EPA based the Strategy on reducing the cumulative risks from all sources of air toxics, including mobile sources.

EPA set 1990 as the base year against which to measure progress in reducing risks in urban areas to be consistent with the 1990 CAA Amendments, which called for reductions in ambient concentrations below those "currently experienced." The Strategy provided four approaches to assess progress in meeting its goals: (1) emissions or ambient concentration weighting; (2) comparisons between ambient concentrations and risk-based concentrations; (3) comparisons between estimated exposures and risk-based concentrations that may yield quantitative estimates of risk; and (4) quantitative estimates of carcinogenic risk for individuals and populations.

The CAA did not mandate a timeframe for achieving the Strategy's goals. However, the CAA called for EPA to submit two reports to Congress on its efforts to address urban air toxics – one each in 1998 and 2002. These reports were to specifically identify urban areas that continued to experience high risks to public health from area source emissions.

EPA Must Also Control Air Toxics Emissions from Mobile Sources

Mobile source emissions are a significant contributor to health risks from exposure to air toxics risks in urban areas. Accordingly, EPA's Integrated Urban Air Toxics Strategy describes actions mandated under CAA Section

202 to reduce air toxics emissions, including diesel particulate matter, from mobile sources. EPA issued regulations in 2001 and 2007 to meet the Act's mandates.

The 2001 rule identified 21 specific pollutants as mobile source air toxics to be evaluated further for potential emission controls. The list of mobile source air toxics includes 20 air toxics identified and regulated under CAA Section 112, as well as diesel exhaust.[2] The 2001 rule did not set any specific vehicle-based standards because EPA determined that the controls in place for other existing mobile source rules represented the most stringent controls available at that time.

In 2007, EPA issued a second mobile source air toxics rule, which set standards for portable fuel containers, hydrocarbon emissions from passenger vehicles, and the benzene content of gasoline. This rule was expected to significantly reduce emissions of several air toxics, including benzene, 1,3-butadiene, and formaldehyde.

EPA has issued other mobile source rules – designed to reduce emissions of criteria pollutants such as nitrogen oxides and particulate matter – that have also reduced air toxics, including the Tier 2 standards for light-duty passenger vehicles. EPA has also issued rules designed to specifically reduce diesel exhaust emissions. These rules include standards for heavy-duty on-road diesel engines, non-road diesel engines, and locomotives and marine vessels.

Prior Audit Reports

U.S. Government Accountability Office (GAO) and EPA Office of Inspector General (OIG) reports identifying problems in regulating air toxics date to 1991. These reports identified problems such as missed deadlines, unreliable emission inventories, insufficient ambient air toxics data, and inadequate funding. Appendix B lists the GAO and OIG reports that we reviewed.

In multiple reports, GAO reported that EPA missed statutory deadlines for air toxics activities, including regulations to reduce air toxics emissions. In April 2000, GAO reported that EPA had met 117 statutory requirements related to air toxics, but 102 of them were met late. In May 2005, GAO reported that EPA had met 216 statutory requirements related to air toxics, but 195 of them were met late. In its most recent report on air toxics, issued in 2006, GAO reported that a large number of statutory requirements remained for EPA to meet, including (1) setting 54 area source standards, (2) conducting more than 90 reviews of the

---

[2] Diesel exhaust is not listed among the air toxics to be regulated under CAA Section 112. However, diesel exhaust contains several regulated air toxics and EPA has concluded it is likely to be a carcinogen. EPA listed diesel exhaust – including diesel particulate matter – as a mobile source air toxic in the 2001 Mobile Source Air Toxics Rule, promulgated pursuant to CAA Section 202(l).

residual health risks from existing MACT standards and issuing additional standards as necessary, and (3) reviewing and updating the list of regulated air toxics as appropriate.

Over the years, GAO has found the air toxics program to be challenged by funding constraints. In reports covering several funding periods ranging from 1991 to 2005, GAO found that inadequate funding for the air toxics program contributed to EPA's inability to meet statutory deadlines, including the issuance of MACT standards. The most recent GAO report, issued in June 2006, reported that EPA's limited progress in implementing the air toxics program was in part due to the air toxics program's lower priority relative to other air programs (e.g., criteria pollutants) and related funding constraints.

A March 2004 OIG report noted that unreliable emissions inventories hindered EPA's ability to accurately measure the progress of its air toxics program. This report noted that States were not required to verify their reported emission inventories, and that changes in the methodologies for developing emission inventories made it difficult to compare current inventories with past inventories.

In March 2005, the OIG reported on EPA's progress in monitoring ambient concentrations of air toxics. Ambient monitoring measures national and local air toxics concentrations. Such monitoring is needed to detect and/or verify areas of unhealthy air toxics concentrations and to help assess progress in reducing air toxics-related health risks by measuring national and local trends in air toxics concentrations. We reported that there were gaps in existing monitoring coverage with respect to areas with high estimated cancer risks and with respect to certain air toxics that are believed to present the largest risks to the most people. We recommended, among other things, that EPA prioritize the award of monitoring grants to areas estimated to have the highest public health risks from exposure to air toxics. EPA agreed to implement this recommendation and revised its grant selection criteria to include the degree of public health risk.

Our October 2007 report on the progress of MACT standards in reducing air toxics emissions concluded that air toxics emissions had decreased after implementing MACT rules, but noted that unreliable emission inventories continued to hinder EPA's ability to measure the program's effectiveness. This report repeated our earlier recommendation that EPA establish mandatory reporting requirements for air toxics emission data. EPA agreed that establishing air toxics emissions reporting requirements could improve the quality of emissions inventory data. However, in September 2009, after consulting with its Office of General Counsel, the Agency commented that it does "not believe the CAA provides EPA with the authority to require states to collect and report HAP emissions data as a part of the Air Emissions Reporting Requirements (AERR)." Thus, the Agency plans to continue to rely on voluntary efforts to obtain air toxics emissions inventory data. The recommendation remains unresolved.

Noteworthy Achievements

EPA launched the Community Action for a Renewed Environment (CARE) program in Fiscal Year (FY) 2005. CARE is a competitive grant program through which local organizations, such as nonprofits, businesses, schools, and governments, create broad-based partnerships to implement local solutions to reduce releases of toxic pollutants and minimize the public's exposure to them. As of January 2010, EPA has awarded 79 CARE grants since 2005. Thirteen grants have been completed, one was returned, and the remaining grants are still active. EPA's reported achievements for the CARE grants include the following:

- All 88 public schools in St. Louis, Missouri, signed up for No Idling Zones, which EPA estimated will save 224,000 gallons of fuel.
- Forty-nine percent of the auto body repair shops visited by the grantee in Tucson, Arizona, participated in a voluntary emissions reduction program, resulting in an estimated decrease of 2,400 to 12,200 pounds per year of solvent emissions.
- Fifteen diesel trucks in Rochester, New York, and 120 school and municipal buses in Pueblo, Colorado, were retrofitted with technologies to reduce air toxics emissions.

Scope and Methodology

To address our objectives, we interviewed staff and managers in EPA's Office of Air Quality Planning and Standards (OAQPS), Office of Transportation and Air Quality, Office of Environmental Justice, and Office of the Chief Financial Officer; and Region 4's Air, Pesticides, Toxics Management Division (the FY 2009 regional sublead for air toxics). We also interviewed staff from the National Association of Clean Air Agencies (NACAA).

We reviewed relevant regulations, reports, and guidance, including Federal Register notices, for all promulgated and proposed area source standards; the 2000 Report to Congress on the Integrated Urban Air Toxics Strategy; mobile source air toxics rules; and EPA's Workplan for the National Air Toxics Program and Integrated Air Toxics State/Local/Tribal Program Structure. In addition, we reviewed data from the 2002 NATA and analyzed these data to determine the estimated percentage of emissions and cancer risk attributable to area sources. We also reviewed data in EPA's Air Toxics Community Assessment and Risk Reduction Projects database, and information pertaining to the CARE projects, Sustainable Skylines projects, and Community-Scale Air Toxics Ambient Monitoring projects.

We conducted our work from May 2009 to March 2010. We conducted this evaluation in accordance with generally accepted government auditing standards. Those standards require that we obtain sufficient, appropriate evidence to provide a reasonable basis for our findings and conclusions based on our evaluation objectives. We believe that the evidence obtained provides a reasonable basis for our findings and conclusions based on our objectives.

Chapter 2
Key CAA-Required Air Toxics Activities Remain Unimplemented

After 10 years, key actions called for by the CAA and outlined in EPA's 1999 Integrated Urban Air Toxics Strategy to address public health risk from exposure to air toxics remain unimplemented. EPA has not determined whether it has the statutory authority to require State and local agencies to implement a federal risk-based program, nor has EPA determined the level of resources needed to fund such a program. Further, a lack of reliable data has contributed to EPA's inability to establish baseline risk data against which to measure progress in reducing the public health risk from exposure to air toxics as required by the CAA. In our opinion, without implementation of a national urban air toxics strategy, State, local agencies, and tribes will not have the necessary programs and resources to meet the public health goals set by Congress for the urban air toxics program. In 2002, about half of the States and several local agencies had laws preventing them from implementing environmental programs that are stricter than EPA's regulations. In the absence of federal risk-based requirements, these State and local agencies may not be able to fully address local areas of high risk. As a result, the public continues to be exposed to levels of air toxics that may cause elevated risks of cancer and other diseases. EPA's last risk assessment, based on 2002 data, estimated that 1 in every 28,000 people could develop cancer from air toxics exposure.

CAA Section 112 Required Urban Air Toxics Strategy

Section 112(k) of the 1990 CAA Amendments required EPA to develop a comprehensive strategy to control emissions of air toxics from area sources in urban areas. The strategy was to identify not less than 30 air toxics emitted from areas sources that present the greatest threat to public health in the largest number of urban areas. Further, the strategy was to identify the source categories emitting these air toxics, and EPA was to ensure that sources accounting for 90 percent or more of the emissions for each of the air toxics were subject to emissions standards. The strategy was to include a schedule of specific actions to substantially reduce the public's health risk from exposure to air toxics emitted by areas sources. Specifically, EPA was to achieve – through implementation of the Strategy – a 75 percent reduction in the incidence of cancer attributable to exposure to air toxics emitted by stationary sources. In addition, EPA was to provide for ambient monitoring and emissions modeling in urban areas as appropriate to demonstrate that the goals and objectives of the strategy were being met.

EPA published the Integrated Urban Air Toxics Strategy in 1999 to address the requirements of CAA 112(k). The Strategy is a major part of EPA's national efforts to reduce air toxics emissions and risk through four key components: stationary and mobile source regulations, cumulative risk initiatives, risk assessment approaches, and education and outreach. The Strategy included plans for EPA to establish appropriate federal measures, through guidance, policies, and rulemaking, to enable State, local, and tribal (S/L/T) agencies to be full partners in implementing a risk-based air toxics program.

CAA Section 112(k) also prescribed additional EPA actions to address area source emissions. In particular, EPA was to encourage local strategies to reduce area source emissions by awarding 10 percent of the funds available for grants under Section 112 to State and local agencies for innovative and effective strategies. EPA was also required to submit two reports to Congress on its actions to reduce public health risks from exposure to air toxics, particularly from area sources. The first report to Congress was required within 8 years of the enactment of the CAA Amendments of 1990 (i.e., by 1998), and the second report was to be completed within 12 years (i.e., by 2002). These reports were to specifically identify metro/urban areas that continue to experience high risks to public health posed by emissions from area sources.

Key CAA Actions Unimplemented

EPA has neither completed key CAA requirements nor implemented key actions outlined in its CAA-required 1999 Strategy to reduce risk in urban areas from air toxics. Specific requirements of the CAA that EPA has not implemented are:

- Promulgating air toxics emissions standards for all area source categories by November 15, 2000.
- Awarding at least 10 percent of funds available under Section 112 to State or local agencies to support strategies to address air toxics emissions from area sources.
- Submitting a second report to Congress on actions taken to reduce risks posed by urban air toxics from area sources.

Specific actions that EPA outlined in its Strategy that it has not implemented include:

- Establishing a minimum risk-based air toxics program for S/L/T agencies.
- Measuring and tracking progress in meeting the Strategy's goals.
- Defining the term "substantial reduction" to track progress in reducing noncancer health impacts.

Air Toxics Emissions Standards Still Needed for Four Area Source Categories

EPA is 10 years behind schedule in promulgating regulations to reduce emissions from area sources in urban areas. EPA was required to promulgate regulations for listed area sources within 10 years of the CAA Amendments of 1990 (i.e., by November 15, 2000). In 2002, EPA completed the required list of area source categories. This list contained 70 area source categories representing at least 90 percent of the area source emissions for each of the 30 air toxics listed in the Strategy. As of January 2010, EPA had promulgated 43 emission standards addressing 66 of the 70 listed area source categories.[3] EPA had not completed standards for the remaining four area source categories.

In addition to issuing area source standards well after their CAA-required implementation dates, many of these standards do not require any additional emission reductions. NACAA has criticized the lack of required emission reductions in EPA's area source rules. In a 2008 report,[4] NACAA noted that some of EPA's area source rules do not require additional controls or merely codify what some State and local agencies already require. NACAA recommended that EPA revisit the area source standards for air toxics and "revise the most deficient ones so that they will result in real reductions in emissions and the associated risks." At least 18 of the 43 area source standards EPA has issued are not expected to result in any additional reductions in air toxics emissions. According to the Federal Register notices for these rules, the most common reason for the lack of expected emission reductions was that the area source category was already well controlled or had already reduced emissions since the enactment of 1990 CAA Amendments.

Effective implementation and enforcement of these rules is also a concern. As noted by NACAA in its December 2008 report, many State and local agencies do not have sufficient resources to take delegation of the area source standards.[5] In its comments to EPA on specific area source rules, NACAA stated EPA should provide sufficient additional funds for the area source rules to be implemented properly. NACAA explained that area sources programs were not eligible for Title V fees and thus would require a significant increase in resources beyond what was currently provided.

---

[3] Some emission standards cover more than one area source category; thus, the number of standards is less than the number of source categories.

[4] NACAA, *Change is in the Air: Recommendations from the National Association of Clean Air Agencies to President-Elect Obama's Administration on Improving Our Nation's Clean Air Program*, December 16, 2008.

[5] EPA environmental programs are generally implemented by the States, local agencies, and tribes through a formal delegation process. In general, an S/L/T agency must demonstrate adequate legal authorities and resources to receive delegation of federal standards. EPA helps fund the S/L/T administration of these programs through program grants.

Absent delegation to States, local agencies, and tribes, EPA will be responsible for implementing these standards. Based on the large number of rules that do not require additional emission reductions and a lack of State resources to implement these rules, we believe these rules may not sufficiently reduce air toxics emissions and risks in urban areas to meet the statutory goals of the Strategy.

EPA Funding for Emission Reduction Strategies Below the CAA Minimum

EPA has not met the CAA's requirement that EPA award at least 10 percent of the grant funds available under CAA Section 112 to support State or local agency area-wide strategies to address air toxics emissions from area sources. According to Section 112(k)(4), these funds should be awarded on a demonstration basis to State and local agencies with innovative and effective strategies.

EPA has not received a separate appropriation for Section 112 grants or activities. Rather, Congress has appropriated funds for air programs under CAA Sections 103 and 105, neither of which carries a 10 percent set-aside requirement for area source strategies. EPA allocates funds under Section 103 and 105 grants to State and local agencies for Section 112 (i.e., air toxics) activities. EPA has allocated roughly $40 million a year in grant funds to State and local agencies for toxics programs from FY 2005 to FY 2010.[6] Thus, to meet the CAA's 10 percent requirement, about $4 million a year should be specifically awarded for projects to reduce area source emissions to meet the CAA requirement. While EPA has awarded grants to State and local agencies for various air toxics-related projects, these grants do not meet the 10 percent requirement for innovative area source reduction strategies.

From FY 2001 to FY 2004, the Office of Air and Radiation (OAR) provided grants for the Community Assessment and Risk Reduction Initiative. This initiative provided approximately $2 million to 30 projects over the course of 4 years. The majority of these projects provided money for pilot demonstration projects designed to assist S/L/T agencies and communities in characterizing their local air toxics problems, developing reduction activities to address those problems, and measuring reductions as they occur. EPA discontinued the initiative after 2004.

Starting in FY 2005, EPA has awarded grants to communities to address public health risks from multiple sources, including air toxics, through the CARE program. There are two levels of CARE grants. First-level projects provide up to $100,000 for planning, partnership development, investigation of toxics, and consensus building on the community's toxic priorities. Second-level projects provide up to $300,000 to carry out strategies to reduce the toxics identified and prioritized in the first level. From FY 2005 to FY 2008, 69 grants were awarded

---

[6] In FY 2007, the allocation was only about $31 million because the budget for that year did not provide any funding for the National Air Toxics Trends Network or community-scale air toxics monitoring.

under CARE. Of the 13 completed CARE grants, 4 identified area source emissions as a community concern and/or addressed these emissions. EPA provided $2 million to fund the CARE program in FY 2009, an amount equal to roughly 5 percent of the funding provided to State and local agency air toxics programs, or about half of the 10 percent required by CAA Section 112(k)(4). Thus, even if all of the CARE projects were focused on reducing emissions from area sources, the total funding would not meet the CAA-required 10 percent funding level.

Second Report to Congress Has Not Been Submitted

EPA has not submitted a second report to Congress on the actions taken under Section 112(k) and other parts of the CAA to reduce risks to public health posed by air toxics from area sources. EPA submitted the first report to Congress in July 2000, 2 years after the deadline specified by the CAA. The second report to Congress, due in 2002, was never written. These reports were to specifically identify urban areas that continue to experience high risks to public health posed by emissions from area sources; however, the first report did not include such a list. In the first report, EPA said it was unable to identify the urban areas that continued to experience high risks to public health as a result of emissions from area sources because it had only recently begun to implement its Strategy. EPA reported that it would be better able to identify those urban areas with high air toxics risks in the following few years as it made progress toward the goals of the Strategy.

Since the first report was issued, EPA has conducted assessments to identify high-risk urban areas. However, EPA has not formally identified these areas for the purpose of establishing a baseline to track progress in meeting the goals of the Strategy.

EPA Has Not Established a Risk-Based Air Toxics Program

As of January 2010, EPA had not established a minimum risk-based air toxics program at the S/L/T levels. While not required by the CAA, EPA had decided such a program was necessary to meet the goals of its Strategy. In its September 2001 work plan for implementing the national air toxics program, EPA set a milestone of 2003 for completing this action.[7]

OAQPS managers and staff told us that they worked with State and local air representatives to develop such a program. OAR concluded that a program was not established in large part because Section 112 of the CAA did not give EPA explicit authority to require such a program. However, OAR's conclusion has not been reviewed or endorsed by EPA's counsel.

---

[7] EPA, OAQPS, Emission Standards Division, *U.S. Environmental Protection Agency Workplan for the National Air Toxics Program and Integrated Air Toxics State/Local/Tribal Program Structure*, September 2001.

If EPA developed an S/L/T risk-based program, OAR would have to address the amount and sources of funding for such a program. In addition, the program would have to address acceptable or unacceptable levels of risks and at what level S/L/T entities should take action to address cumulative risks in urban areas. As of January 2010, EPA had not established any action levels for addressing cancer and noncancer risks in local communities.

While some States and local agencies have implemented their own risk-based air toxics programs independently of EPA, according to a 2002 survey by NACAA, about half of the States and several local agencies[8] had laws preventing them from implementing environmental regulations that were stricter than EPA's regulations. In the absence of federal risk-based requirements, these States and local agencies may not be able to fully address local areas of high risk. Thus, without the establishment of a minimum, federally required risk-based program, we do not believe that all States and local agencies will be able to implement programs to adequately address the health risks from urban air toxics.

EPA Has Not Tracked Progress for Meeting the Strategy's Goals

EPA has not tracked its progress in meeting the goals of the Strategy. EPA has implemented over 100 air toxics rules[9] since the 1990 CAA Amendments, and data indicate that air toxics emissions have decreased accordingly. However, as described in the Strategy, tracking cumulative risk from exposure to air toxics would require EPA to move its performance tracking focus from emissions reductions to reductions in cancer and noncancer health risks. EPA has made some progress in this area, as its current performance measures for the national air toxics program are based on reductions in toxicity-weighted emissions. The current performance measures are an improvement over gross emissions reductions measures in that they weight the reductions based on their toxicity. However, this approach lacks the dispersion and exposure modeling steps of an exposure assessment and therefore cannot provide quantitative estimates of risk. Such quantitative estimates of risk are needed to assess whether the goals of the Strategy are being met.

EPA planned to use a quantitative risk-based approach to assess its progress in meeting the goals of the Strategy starting with the 1996 emission inventory,[10] which would be the first year the inventory included the point-specific

---

[8] According to a 2002 survey conducted by NACAA (formerly STAPPA/ALAPCO), 26 States and 9 local agencies responded that they were either partially or totally prohibited from implementing air programs that are more stringent than the federal program.

[9] These rules include MACT standards and residual risk rules for major sources, as well as GACT standards for area sources.

[10] EPA develops an air toxics emission inventory, known as the National Emission Inventory, every 3 years. Emissions data from the National Emission Inventory are input into the models used for NATA.

information needed to model ambient toxics concentrations.[11] EPA has conducted three quantitative assessments of national air toxics risk (i.e., NATA) based on emissions data for 1996, 1999, and 2002. However, EPA has not used these assessments to establish baseline risk data for measuring progress. According to EPA's NATA Website, it is not meaningful to compare the results between assessments because any changes in emissions, ambient concentrations, or risks may be due to either improvement in methodology or to real changes in emissions. Further, EPA's NATA Website states that the NATA results should be used cautiously because the quality and uncertainties of the assessments vary from location to location, as well as from pollutant to pollutant. In addition, point-specific emissions data for area sources are very limited.

Accordingly, EPA must use models to estimate the types and numbers of area sources in a given location. According to EPA staff, this type of modeling estimate accounts for 95 percent of area source emissions used as input into NATA. Thus, the accuracy of the area source emissions inventories is even more uncertain than the major source inventories. As a result, EPA does not have a process for assessing its progress in meeting the goals of the Strategy.

Key Terms Undefined

EPA has not defined key terms needed to establish measures for the goals outlined in the Strategy. Specifically, EPA has not defined or quantified the term "substantial reduction" for Goal No. 2 of the Strategy. The CAA and EPA's Strategy specify a substantial reduction in public health risks for effects other than cancer, but EPA has not defined substantial. The Strategy states that EPA intended to use information from its initial noncancer risk assessment to develop a more complete and quantitative goal for a substantial reduction in noncancer risk. As of August 2009, EPA had conducted three noncancer risk assessments as part of its three NATA assessments, but had still not defined what it means to obtain a substantial reduction in noncancer risk.

The Strategy also includes the goal of addressing disproportionate impacts of air toxics hazards across urban areas such as geographic "hot spots," highly exposed population subgroups, and predominately minority and low-income communities. As of August 2009, EPA had not (1) defined geographic hot spots, (2) defined what constitutes disproportionate impacts, (3) systemically identified areas subject to disproportionate impacts, or (4) decided how to address these areas. Based on the results of EPA's 2002 NATA, many urban areas are likely still experiencing excessive risks from air toxics. Specifically, EPA estimates that in 2002, about 2 million Americans lived in areas with excess lifetime cancer risks from exposure to air toxics greater than 1 in 10,000. Cancer risks in excess of 1 in 10,000 are generally considered unacceptable by EPA.

---

[11] A point-specific or "model-ready" inventory records the latitude and longitude of stationary sources of emissions. The exact locations of the emissions sources are needed as inputs for models that estimate ambient air concentrations resulting from these emissions.

The fact that these key terms remain undefined after 10 years suggests a lack of attention to implementing the Strategy.

Conclusions

Since 1990, EPA has issued over 100 rules to address air toxics emissions, and data indicate that air toxics emissions have decreased. However, public health risks from exposures to air toxics remain a concern, particularly in urban areas that can experience concentrated emissions of air toxics. EPA developed its Integrated Urban Air Toxics Strategy to carry out the 1990 CAA Amendments more than 10 years ago; yet key actions called for by the CAA and outlined in EPA's Strategy remain unimplemented. Given the length of time since the Strategy was developed and the problems EPA has encountered in implementing the Strategy, EPA should reassess and update its approach to addressing urban air toxics. The absence of an effective EPA strategy adversely affects the ability of other entities to address local conditions. As a result, many communities may continue to experience elevated health risks from exposure to air toxics.

Recommendations

We recommend that the Assistant Administrator for Air and Radiation:

2-1   Develop and submit the required second Urban Air Toxics Report to Congress by the end of FY 2010. This report should:

    a. Disclose the current status and progress made in meeting Section 112(k) of the CAA.

    b. Identify the urban areas that continue to experience high or unacceptable health risks from cancer and noncancer effects, and how EPA plans to reduce risks in these areas.

    c. Address the major factors that have hindered implementation of the Integrated Urban Air Toxics Strategy, and how EPA plans to address these factors.

    d. Provide details on how the Agency intends to meet the CAA Section 112(k) requirement that at least 10 percent of Section 112 funds to go to State or local agencies to support strategies to address air toxics emissions from area sources.

    e. Disclose air toxics requirements that the Agency is unable to meet through its current authorities.

2-2   Determine how the Agency will measure progress in meeting the goals of the Strategy. If the Assistant Administrator determines that the development and maintenance of a 1990 or similar baseline is not cost effective, EPA should develop and inform Congress of the Agency's alternative measures for assessing its progress in meeting the intent of the statutory goals.

Agency Comments and OIG Evaluation

OAR generally agreed with our findings and conclusions in its May 11, 2010, written response, with some exceptions. OAR partially agreed with the report's recommendations.

Regarding Recommendation 2-1, OAR agreed to include a discussion of the specific items listed in the statute in its second report to Congress, but did not agree to include a discussion of the additional issues we recommended. We believe EPA should include a discussion of these topics as listed in our recommendation (a list of urban areas that continue to experience high or unacceptable levels of risk, how EPA plans to reduce risks in those areas, the factors that have hindered implementation of the Strategy, and how EPA plans to address those factors) in its second report to Congress, because we believe these issues are contributing factors to delayed implementation of the statute, and they would more fully inform Congress of the status of the program.

Regarding Recommendation 2-2, OAR agreed to determine how it would measure progress in meeting the goals of the Strategy. However, OAR did not agree to inform Congress of this plan if it involves measuring progress against an alternative to a 1990 or similar baseline. The 1990 CAA Amendments stated that EPA should reduce ambient concentrations in large urban areas to levels substantially below those currently experienced (i.e., 1990). Accordingly, we believe Congress should be informed if the Agency's measurement system does not use a baseline reflecting conditions experienced at the time the CAA Amendments were passed. We revised our recommendation by replacing the phrase "pre-CAA baseline" with "1990 or similar baseline" to clarify the intent of our recommendation.

At our June 17, 2010, exit conference, the Agency said it would reassess its approach to the recommendations in preparing its corrective action plan in response to the final report. We consider the recommendations unresolved. They will remain open in our tracking system pending our receipt and analysis of the Agency's 90-day corrective action plan. See Appendices C and D for the Agency's response to our draft report and our more detailed evaluation of that response.

Status of Recommendations and Potential Monetary Benefits

		RECOMMENDATIONS				POTENTIAL MONETARY BENEFITS (in $000s)	
Rec. No.	Page No.	Subject	Status[1]	Action Official	Planned Completion Date	Claimed Amount	Agreed To Amount
2-1	16	Develop and submit the required second Urban Air Toxics Report to Congress by the end of FY 2010. This report should: a. Disclose the current status and progress made in meeting Section 112(k) of the CAA. b. Identify the urban areas that continue to experience high or unacceptable health risks from cancer and noncancer effects, and how EPA plans to reduce risks in these areas. c. Address the major factors that have hindered implementation of the Integrated Urban Air Toxics Strategy, and how EPA plans to address these factors. d. Provide details on how the Agency intends to meet the CAA Section 112(k) requirement that at least 10 percent of Section 112 funds to go to State or local agencies to support strategies to address air toxics emissions from area sources. e. Disclose air toxics requirements that the Agency is unable to meet through its current authorities.	U	Assistant Administrator for Air and Radiation			
2-2	17	Determine how the Agency will measure progress in meeting the goals of the Strategy. If the Assistant Administrator determines that the development and maintenance of a 1990 or similar baseline is not cost effective, EPA should develop and inform Congress of the Agency's alternative measures for assessing its progress in meeting the intent of the statutory goals.	U	Assistant Administrator for Air and Radiation			

[1] O = recommendation is open with agreed-to corrective actions pending
    C = recommendation is closed with all agreed-to actions completed
    U = recommendation is undecided with resolution efforts in progress

Appendix A

EPA's Estimates of Risks from Exposure to Air Toxics

In its latest NATA, EPA estimated that nearly all of the 285 million people in the United States (based on the 2000 census) had an increased cancer risk of greater than 10 in 1 million from exposure to air toxics.[12] The average cancer risk for 2002 was 36 in 1 million. Therefore, on average, approximately 1 in every 28,000 people could develop cancer as a result of breathing air toxics from outdoor sources with a lifetime of exposure to 2002 emission levels. Further, 2 million people had an increased cancer risk of greater than 100 in 1 million. Of the 86 air toxics showing potential cancer risks, benzene was the most significant, contributing to about 30 percent of the overall average risk. Another large contributor to the overall average cancer risk was carbon tetrachloride, which accounted for about 20 percent of the cancer risk. Figure A-1 displays the estimated county-level carcinogenic risk for the United States in 2002. Since the figure is based on countywide averages, the public health risks in some neighborhoods may be higher or lower than depicted in the figure.

Figure A-1: Summary Risk Map for U.S. Carcinogenic Risk at the County Level, 2002

Source: EPA Summary of Results for the 2002 NATA.

---

[12] NATA does not include diesel exhaust emissions in its cancer risk assessments because of a lack of sufficient data for EPA to set a unit risk estimate for diesel exhaust.

EPA also estimated the number of people with the potential to experience adverse noncancer neurological and respiratory health effects, as represented by a hazard index greater than 1.0. A hazard index at or below 1.0 will likely not result in adverse noncancer health effects over a lifetime of exposure, and a hazard index greater than 1.0 can be best described as indicating that a potential may exist for adverse health effects.[13]

Based on the 2002 NATA, the majority of the United States was below a hazard index of 1.0 for neurological effects. However, the majority of the U.S. population experienced a hazard index above 1.0 for respiratory effects. Of the 43 air toxics showing the potential for respiratory effects, acrolein was the most significant, contributing almost 90 percent of the nationwide average noncancer hazard. Sources of acrolein include tobacco smoke, forest fires, and the burning of fuels such as gasoline and oil. Figure A-2 displays the county-level respiratory hazard index in the United States for 2002. Since the figure is based on countywide averages, the hazard index in some neighborhoods may be higher or lower than depicted in the figure.

Figure A-2: Summary Risk Map for U.S. Respiratory Noncancer Risk at the County Level, 2002

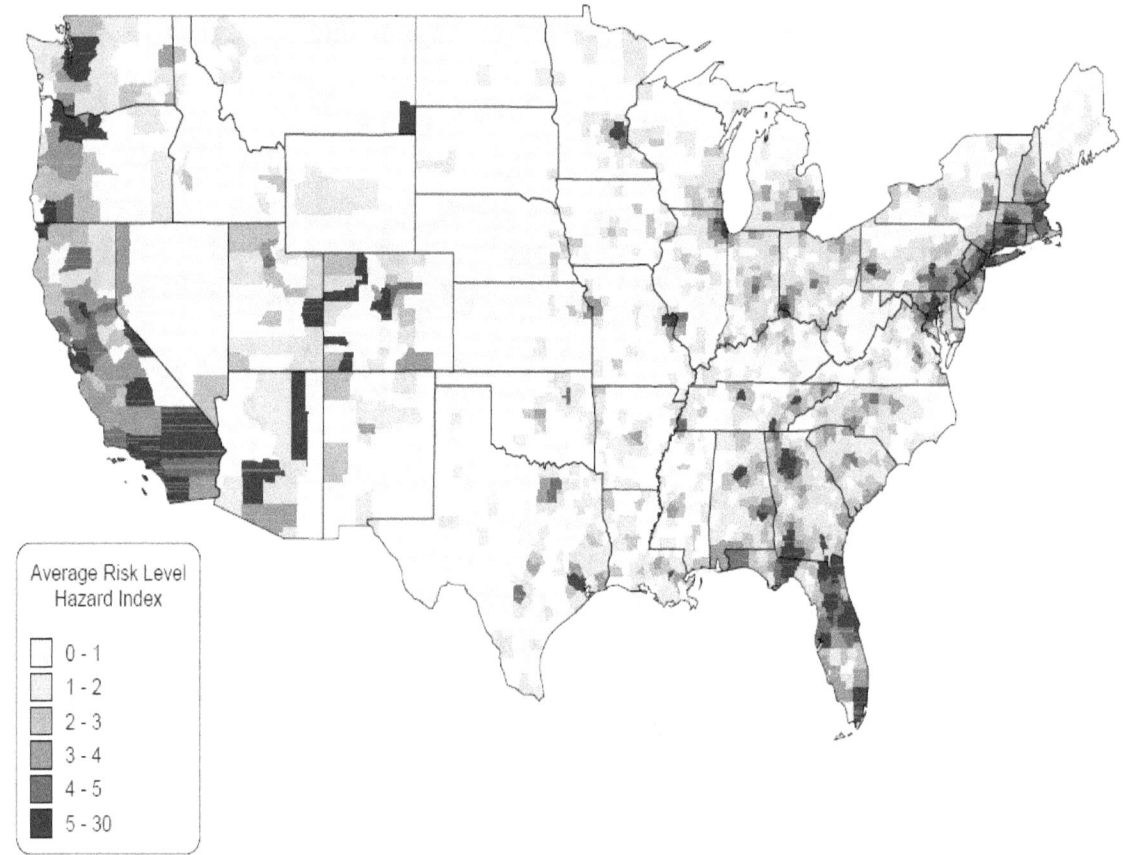

Source: EPA Summary of Results for the 2002 NATA.

---

[13] A hazard index greater than 1.0 does not necessarily suggest an increased likelihood of adverse effects. Additionally, the hazard index cannot be translated to a probability that adverse effects will occur, and is not likely to be proportional to risk.

Sources of the Risks from Air Toxics

Based on the 2002 NATA results, background concentrations accounted for about half (46 percent) of the overall U.S. average cancer risk. The background concentrations are composed of air toxics for which there are currently no known emission sources but that may be detected in the ambient air by monitors. These background concentrations can result from the transport of air toxics from other areas, unidentified emission sources, and natural emission sources.

EPA estimated that mobile sources (i.e., on-road and non-road sources) and area sources accounted for about 30 percent and 18 percent, respectively, of the overall U.S. average cancer risk. The remaining 6 percent of the estimated risk was from major sources. Figure A-3 shows the percentage contribution from each sector to the overall estimated cancer risk in the United States.

Figure A-3: Percentage Cancer Risk Contribution by Source Sector, 2002

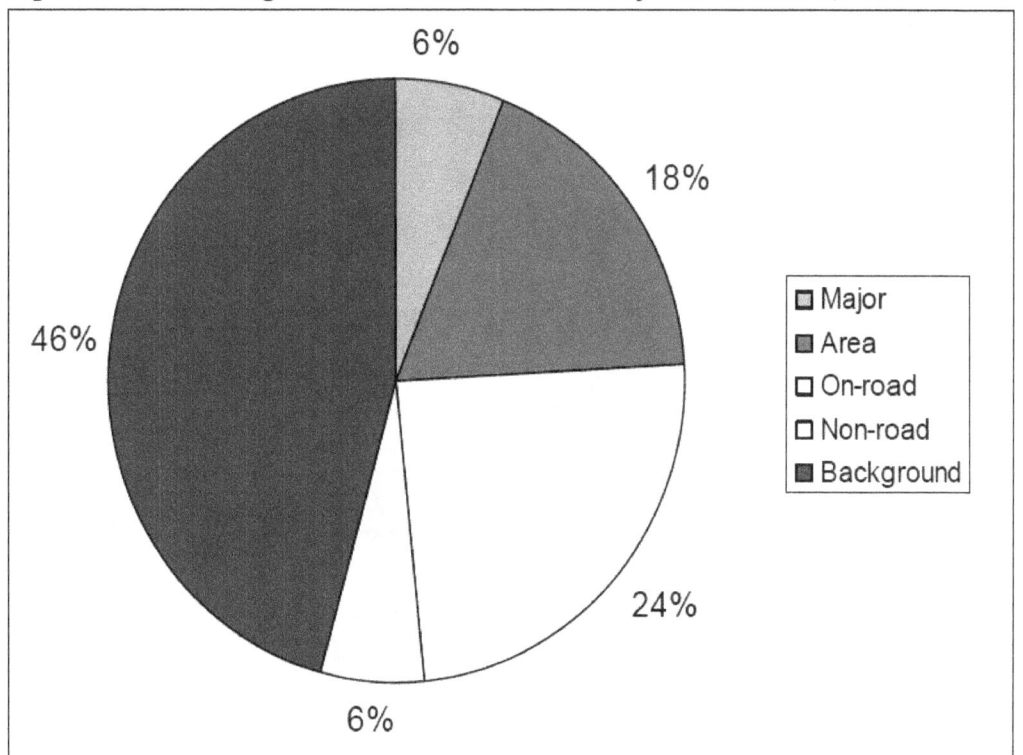

Source: OIG figure based on 2002 NATA data.

For noncancer adverse health effects, the 2002 NATA results show that mobile sources (i.e., on-road and non-road sources) were the most significant source for potential respiratory impacts, contributing about 78 percent of the overall nationwide average respiratory noncancer hazard index. Area sources accounted for about 18 percent of the overall U.S. average respiratory noncancer hazard index. Figure A-4 shows the percentage contribution from each source sector to the overall U.S. estimated hazard index for respiratory noncancer effects.

Figure A-4: Percentage Respiratory Hazard Index Contribution by Source Sector, 2002

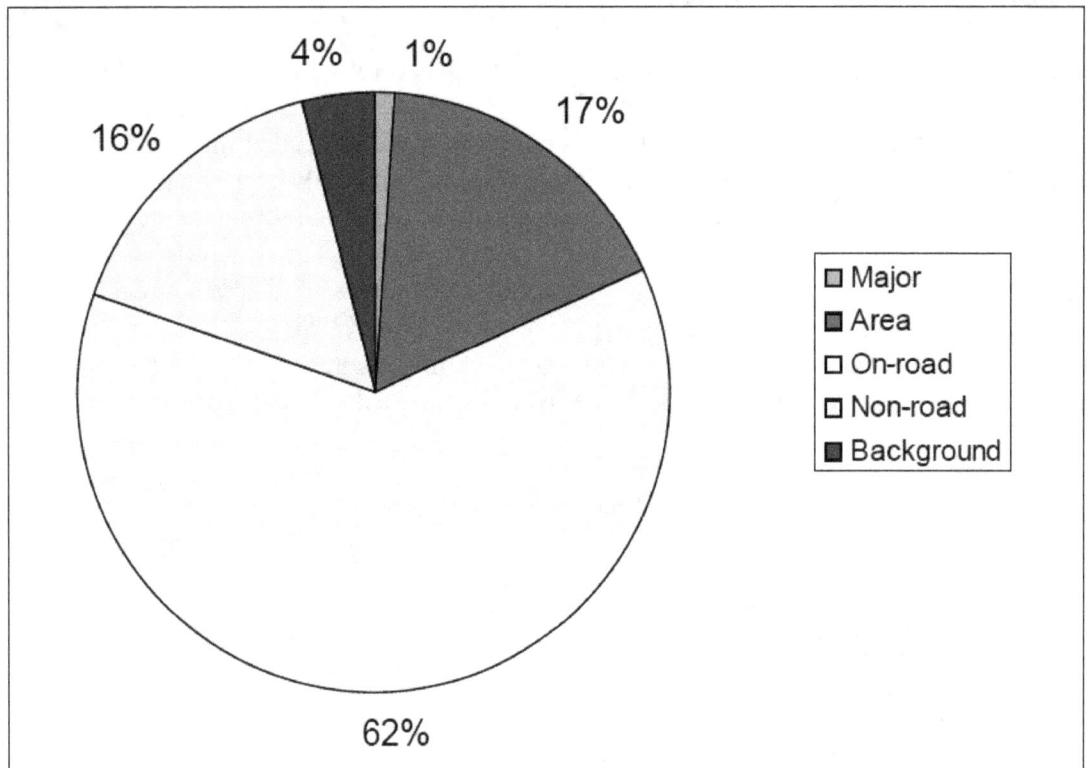

Source: OIG figure based on 2002 NATA data.

Prior GAO and EPA OIG Audit Reports

We reviewed the following GAO and EPA OIG reports related to EPA's air toxics program:

GAO

- *Air Pollution: EPA's Strategy and Resources May be Inadequate to Control Air Toxics.* GAO/RCED-91-143, June 26, 1991.
- *Air Pollution: Progress and Problems in Implementing Selected Aspects of the Clean Air Act Amendments of 1990.* GAO/T-RCED-94-68, October 29, 1993.
- *Air Pollution: Reductions in EPA's 1994 Air Quality Program's Budget.* GAO/RCED-95-31BR, November 29, 1994.
- *Air Pollution: Status of Implementation and Issues of the Clean Air Act Amendments of 1990.* GAO/RCED-00-72, April 17, 2000.
- *Clean Air Act: EPA Has Completed Most of the Actions Required by the 1990 Amendments, but Many Were Completed Late.* GAO-05-613, May 27, 2005.
- *Clean Air Act: EPA Should Improve the Management of Its Air Toxics Program.* GAO-06-669, June 23, 2006.

EPA OIG

- *Clean Air Design Evaluation Results.* Report No. 2002-M-000013, April 23, 2002.
- *EPA's Methods for Calculating Air Toxics Emissions for Reporting Results Needs Improvement.* Report No. 2004-P-00012, March 31, 2004.
- *Progress Made in Monitoring Ambient Air Toxics, But Further Improvements Can Increase Effectiveness.* Report No. 2005-P-00008, March 2, 2005.
- *Improvements in Air Toxics Emissions Data Needed to Conduct Residual Risk Assessments.* Report No. 08-P-0020, October 31, 2007.

Agency Comments

May 11, 2010

<u>MEMORANDUM</u>

SUBJECT: Response to Draft Evaluation Report: "Key Activities in EPA's Integrated
                         Urban Air Toxics Strategy Remain Unimplemented," Project No.
                         OPE FY09-0008

FROM: Gina McCarthy
                         Assistant Administrator

TO: Wade T. Najjum
                         Assistant Inspector General for Program Evaluation

This is in response to your March 30, 2010, draft evaluation report titled, "Key Activities in EPA's Integrated Urban Air Toxics Strategy Remain Unimplemented." Thank you for the opportunity to review the report and provide comment. As noted in the report, you assessed how EPA tracks progress with three goals of the Urban Air Toxics Strategy (the Strategy). These goals are:

- Attaining a 75 percent reduction in cancer incidence attributable to exposure to hazardous air pollutants (HAP) emitted by large and small stationary sources nationwide;
- Attaining a substantial reduction in public health risks (such as birth defects and reproduction effects) posed by HAP emissions from small industrial/commercial sources known as area sources; and
- Addressing disproportionate impacts from air toxics across urban areas, such as geographic "hot spots," highly exposed population subgroups, and predominately minority and low-income communities.

As you are aware, the Urban Air Toxics Strategy comprises four components: source-specific and sector-based emission standards; national, regional, and community-based initiatives; air toxics assessment; and education and outreach. EPA has made significant strides in reducing emissions of HAP through both its regulatory and non-regulatory actions conducted under the authority of the Clean Air Act (CAA) Section 112. Despite this progress, we agree that much remains to be done to ensure healthy, clean air for all Americans, particularly those living in urban areas where emission sources can be more concentrated and those living in communities near facilities emitting HAP. Urban areas are impacted by major and area stationary sources, as well as mobile sources. We are making significant progress in understanding the contributions these sources make toward our health risk, and we have achieved noteworthy reductions in emissions of these pollutants since the CAA amendments of 1990.

Note that throughout this memorandum, we will be using the terms HAP and air toxics interchangeably.

Overview of Accomplishments, Challenges and Funding Issues

EPA has made significant strides in reducing air toxics. As highlighted in EPA's recent report titled, "Our Nation's Air,"[14] we are making progress at a majority of sites in the U.S. in reducing concentrations of important air toxics. The ambient monitoring data described in that report show that the concentrations of some of the HAP of greatest widespread concern to public health (i.e., 1,3-butadiene, benzene, tetrachloroethylene, and 1,4-dichlorobenzene) are declining at most monitoring sites. Concentrations of volatile organic compounds (VOCs) such as 1,3-butadiene, benzene, styrene, xylenes, and toluene decreased by approximately 5 percent or more per year at more than half of all monitoring sites. Chlorinated VOCs such as tetrachloroethylene, dichloromethane, and methyl chloroform decreased at more than half of all monitoring sites between 2000 and 2005 (the most recent years of ambient air quality data with which to make such assessments).

As noted in the March 30, 2010, Draft Evaluation Report titled, "Key Activities in EPA's Integrated Urban Air Toxics Strategy Remain Unimplemented" (the draft report), EPA has issued 96 maximum achievable control technology (MACT) standards covering all the 174 major source categories originally listed in 1992, as required by the CAA. We have also issued final area source standards for all but three of the source categories that are necessary to meet the 90 percent requirement in section 112(c)(3). Recently, on April 29, 2010, the Administrator signed a proposed rule covering two of the listed area source categories (i.e., Industrial Boilers and Commercial/Institutional Boilers). Also, on April 29, 2010, the Administrator signed proposed standards for Industrial, Commercial, and Institutional Boilers located at major sources (Boiler MACT rule) and Commercial, Institutional and Solid Waste Incineration sources (CISWI rule).[15] We are under a court-ordered deadline for the Administrator to sign final emission standards for these categories by December 16, 2010. Further, we intend to issue final emission standards for Sewage Sludge Incinerators by December 16, 2010. At that point, measured from the 1990 baseline inventory, we will have established standards for the sources that account for at least 90 percent of the emissions of the urban air toxic pollutants. We also intend to complete emission standards for those sources that account for at least 90 percent of the six bio-accumulative toxic pollutants identified in Section 112(c)(6) by December 16, 2010. We project that over two million fewer tons of HAP will be emitted annually than would have occurred in the absence of these major and area stationary source rules.

EPA has also issued regulations that are achieving dramatic reductions in mobile source air toxics (MSATs) from highway vehicles as well as nonroad engines and equipment. We estimate that these rules will reduce emissions of gaseous air toxics from highway mobile sources by about 65 percent between 1999 and 2030, despite large increases in vehicle miles traveled. Similarly, we estimate that such emissions from nonroad equipment will be reduced by about 60 percent between 1999 and 2030. By 2030, we expect to see on-highway diesel

---

[14] http://www.epa.gov/airtrends/2010/
[15] http://www.epa.gov/airquality/combustion/actions.html

particulate matter (PM) emission reductions of over 90 percent from 2001 levels (and over 80 percent reductions for diesel PM from nonroad sources).

These reductions in MSATs result from a series of standards that reduce hydrocarbons from gasoline engines and vehicles, and PM from diesel engines and vehicles. EPA's rule specifically targeted at MSATs was published in 2007 ("Control of Hazardous Air Pollutants from Mobile Sources," or "MSAT2"). That rule has three components: (1) a standard lowering the benzene content of gasoline (beginning in 2011); (2) a standard reducing exhaust emissions from passenger vehicles operating at cold temperatures (under 75 degrees), beginning in 2010; and (3) a standard reducing emissions that evaporate from, and permeate through, portable fuel containers (beginning in 2009). In addition, other regulations that reduce mobile source air toxics include the Tier 2/low-sulfur gasoline standards for light-duty cars and trucks; heavy-duty engine and vehicle standards (including requirements for ultra-low sulfur diesel); and emission standards for nonroad diesel engines, small gasoline engines, recreational marine engines, locomotives, and marine vessels. All these standards have been issued since 2000.

In addition to these national emissions standards that reduce MSAT emissions from new vehicles and engines, EPA also assists States, communities and citizens in identifying and implementing voluntary programs that reduce emissions from the existing fleet. The National Clean Diesel Campaign advances strategies, such as retrofits, to reduce diesel emissions from school buses, truck fleets, ports, and construction sites. EPA is administering $120 million in EPA FY'09 and FY'10 appropriations, and the American Recovery and Reinvestment Act of 2009 provided $300 million in new funding for national and state programs to support the implementation of verified and certified diesel emission reduction technologies.

The MACT standards are our most powerful regulatory tools for reducing HAP from stationary sources. Section 112 of the CAA establishes an ambitious agenda for HAP reduction. EPA must review all MACT and generally available control technology (GACT) standards every eight years pursuant to Section 112(d)(6), and revise those standards as necessary considering developments in practices, processes, and control technologies. We must conduct risk assessments pursuant to Section 112(f)(2) within 8 years of the date of issuance of a MACT standard and determine whether the MACT standard appropriately protects human health with an ample margin of safety. Over the past few years, some MACT rules have been found deficient by the courts, necessitating revisions. When these rules are revised to comply with the court decisions and statutory requirements, we expect them to yield significant additional reductions in emissions, with attendant improvements in public health. It will take time and resources to reissue these rules. EPA has not always been able to keep up with the schedules established in the law, resulting in deadline lawsuits that have often served to set our agenda. Between 2010 and 2012, the office responsible for carrying out the Strategy will have more than 100 regulatory actions at some stage of development, the vast majority of which are either court-ordered or mandated by law.

Despite steady progress, we agree there is more to be done. Unfortunately, limited resources over the past eight years have impaired our ability to fully implement these programs. For example, air toxics support has been cut over 70 percent since FY 2001. For the first time in almost a decade, this year EPA has shifted funds from other programs to help meet regulatory deadlines.

Response to Specific Comments that CAA Actions Remain Unimplemented

We acknowledge your concern about certain CAA-required air toxics activities remaining unimplemented. Listed below are the items which you identified along with our response.

a) Promulgating air toxics standards for area source categories by November 15, 2000.

As noted above, we have a court-ordered deadline to complete by December 16, 2010, emission standards for those area source categories that are necessary to meet the 90 percent requirement in section 112(c)(3). We have completed standards for all of the area source categories, except three. Specifically, we will be issuing emission standards for the boilers and CISWI rules described above and a rule for sewage sludge incinerators by December 16, 2010. We anticipate that these rules, along with the air toxics rule for boilers located at major sources which will be promulgated on the same schedule, will result in significant reductions in emissions of both HAP and criteria pollutants in urban areas.

b) Awarding at least 10 percent of funds available under Section 112 to state or local agencies to support strategies to address air toxics emissions from area sources.

Funds for urban air toxics area-wide strategies have never been appropriated to the Agency by Congress under Section 112 of the Act. Congress has appropriated funds to the Agency under Sections 103 and 105, and the Agency has issued annual program guidance for numerous years encouraging the use of a portion of these funds by recipients to support such activity. However, neither of these authorities carries a 10 percent set-aside requirement. In addition, the Agency has used other avenues to target funds for priority air toxics needs. For example, as noted in the draft report, the Community Action for a Renewed Environment (CARE) program has provided 79 competitive grants, creating broad-based partnerships to implement local solutions to reduce releases of toxic pollutants and minimize public exposure. As outlined in the 2009 National Academy of Public Administration report titled, "Putting Community First: A Promising Approach to Federal Collaboration for Environmental Improvement,"[16] many of these grants have gone to communities in urban areas and many have identified air toxics issues, such as diesel emissions, as among the highest priorities. Prior to implementation of CARE in 2005, OAR awarded grants through the Community Air Risk Reduction Initiative (CARI), with a goal towards enabling communities to better understand local air toxics issues. Ninety grants and other ongoing projects are currently underway and being tracked in a community air toxics database.[17]

The Agency is nearing completion of a monitoring project at 65 schools nationwide, many of which are located in urban areas. This program has been designed to evaluate air toxics

---

[16] http://www napawash.org/pc_management_studies/CARE/5-21-09_Final_Evaluation_Report.pdf
[17] http://yosemite.epa.gov/oar/CommunityAssessment.nsf/Welcome?OpenForm

risks to children and the communities in which they live. OAR has continued to enhance its air toxic monitoring network to look at both national and local issues via the National Air Toxic Trend Sites (NATTS) and the community-scale air toxic monitoring efforts, respectively.

> **c) Submitting a second report to Congress on actions taken to reduce risks posed by urban air toxics from area sources.**

Please refer to our response to the recommendations of the draft report on page 9.

Response to Specific Actions Outlined in EPA's Strategy but not implemented (per the Draft Report)

The following activities identified in your draft report are not required by the statute, but were initially included either in the Strategy or in a work plan EPA issued in 2001 to support state, tribal and local air toxics programs. Our work over this past decade has further refined our thinking about air toxics and ways to reduce public exposure to HAP. As a result, we are now in a better position to re-evaluate the recommendations made in the Strategy and in the September 2001 work plan.

a) Establishing a minimum risk-based air toxics program

Through our experience addressing national air toxics issues over the last 10 years, we believe that establishing a "minimum risk-based air toxics program" may not be the only approach to reducing risks nationwide in urban areas. There are significant complexities associated with developing a minimum risk-based program. Due to the fact that air toxics issues can vary significantly from state to state, as well as community to community, the premise of a "one size fits all" program (i.e., a program that sets risk-based health limits nationwide) may not be the best national approach to reducing risk posed by emissions from numerous and geographically diverse small stationary and mobile sources. As such, we plan to re-examine this approach in conjunction with our development of the 2nd Report to Congress.

While we have not developed a minimum risk-based air toxics program for states, tribes or local agencies, we have helped these agencies by encouraging and supporting their area-wide air toxics strategies. EPA has developed technical support materials to provide guidance and recommendations for conducting risk assessments that can inform the development of such strategies. For example, EPA has developed the Air Toxics Risk Assessment Reference Library, a three volume compendium of state of the art techniques for conducting all types of risk assessments for sources of HAP. In addition, we developed a hands-on train-the-trainer course and delivered it at each of the ten EPA regional offices during 2004 and 2005. The four-day course addressed the use of risk assessment approaches in the development of emission reduction strategies for state, local and tribal air pollution agency personnel. As a result of these technical support and outreach activities, state, tribal and local air pollution agencies are better equipped to use state of the art risk assessment methodologies and develop their own risk-based air pollution control strategies. Many have used risk assessments to inform the development of regulatory and non-regulatory strategies to reduce the health risks associated with HAP.

We recognize that after implementation of our national rules, local air toxics issues may still remain. To help state, tribal and local programs address these local needs, EPA has developed and continues to refine and improve tools such as the National Air Toxics Assessment (NATA), a national assessment of emissions, risk, and exposure to over 100 air toxics. We also use ambient monitoring to identify national and local sources of air toxics risk. Under the residual risk program, we are currently evaluating more holistic risks in the decision-making process by comparing the risks from the specific source category with other local risks, such as those from all air toxics sources within the facility.

An example of an innovative approach to assessing urban air toxics includes a multi-pollutant study completed in Detroit, Michigan, in 2008. This OAR study demonstrated the feasibility of assessing the potential co-benefits from strategies to reduce emissions of both air toxics and criteria pollutants simultaneously. The study demonstrated that the "multi-pollutant, risk-based" approach could: (1) achieve the same or greater reductions of $PM_{2.5}$ and ozone (O_3) at monitors; (2) improve air quality regionally and across the Detroit urban core for multiple pollutants, including HAP; (3) produce approximately two times greater monetized benefits for $PM_{2.5}$ and O_3; (4) reduce non-cancer risk; and (5) result in greater net benefits and be more cost effective. EPA is supporting both a follow-on study similar to the Detroit assessment in another urban area and pilot efforts by state and local governments to prepare a multi-pollutant Air Quality Management Plan (AQMP) to explore the policy issues of implementing this approach.

b) Measuring and tracking progress in meeting the Strategy's goals

While a direct measurement of both cancer and non-cancer health effects and associated risks is not feasible for purposes of establishing a baseline, EPA plans to use other tools as a surrogate to measure progress. Although NATA is the Agency's most complete assessment of the nation's overall cancer and non-cancer air toxics risks, the ability to generate a NATA-like analysis for a pre-1990 "snapshot" is not technically feasible. The site-specific data, such as stack parameters, that are required by the NATA modeling system are not available or were simply not collected in 1990. In lieu of making the many assumptions necessary to complete such an inventory, EPA believes that using other available data as surrogates to measure the change in risk to the public, such as "toxicity-weighted" emission inventory measures, is adequate. EPA is currently using such measures to track program progress under the Office of Management and Budget's Program Assessment Review Tool (PART) annual reporting requirements. EPA believes that such a measure can also serve as a surrogate to measure progress towards the CAA's goal of attaining a 75 percent reduction in the incidence of cancer attributable to exposure to HAP emitted from stationary sources nationwide.

EPA works with states and local governments to continually update and refine NATA. NATA provides comprehensive information on pollutants and emission sources of HAP in every urban area of the country. The next iteration of NATA will be released in summer 2010. NATA has become an important tool to assist the Agency in developing environmental justice profiles and solutions and to identify hot spots or anomalous high values. Compiling and publishing the NATA has encouraged companies to be more aware of their toxics emissions, which is a key initial step to reduction activities.

EPA also increased the effort to better evaluate and understand the current state of urban air toxics. Specifically in 2009, as noted on page 4 of this response, EPA initiated a national air toxics monitoring initiative focusing on 65 schools, many of which are located in cities. This effort was designed to go beyond the NATA analysis and to better understand and characterize the exposure of school children and their communities to air toxics.

In 2011, EPA plans to award as much as $4.9 million in community-scale air toxics monitoring grants thereby providing the opportunity to measure air toxics in communities, including areas around schools, where appropriate. These community grants will focus on many of the urban air toxics issues that the strategy was developed to address. We intend to continue to support the community-scale air toxics monitoring project in the future. Between 2004 and 2008, we awarded grants, which ranged from $50,000 to $750,000, to 53 communities. Funded projects were designed to identify and profile air toxics sources, develop and assess emerging measurement methods, characterize the degree and extent of local air toxics problems, and track progress of air toxics reduction activities.

EPA also operates 27 National Air Toxic Trend Sites (NATTS), 20 of which are located in urban areas. These sites are expected to provide trends data (when the network has five years of representative and acceptable data) to track progress in reducing ambient concentrations. This network represents a $5 million annual commitment to better understand our progress in reducing air toxics in both urban and rural areas.

EPA continues to invest in improvements to emissions inventories for air toxics within the current statutory and regulatory framework. For the 2008 National Emissions Inventory (NEI), EPA's new Emissions Inventory System will store and analyze emissions data for criteria pollutants and HAP. This system will allow for an improved NEI. In an effort to improve the amount and quality of HAP data in 2009, we spent half of our budget for emissions inventory development on HAP emissions. Among other things, we improved coordination of information collection activities associated with rule development, such as the recent boilers/CISWI information collection request, with our emissions inventory "build out."

We have initiated an emissions inventory improvement partnership with the South Coast Air Quality Management District and the California Air Resources Board to use the lessons learned from the 2002 and 2005 NATA emissions inventories to improve reporting of air toxics for both the 2008 NEI and NATA.

One factor that has affected EPA's ability to implement the strategy in the past is the uneven quality of the air toxics emissions inventory. Although data quality has greatly improved over the years since its inception, continued improvements are needed and are underway. One way that EPA is addressing this issue is through its stationary source rules for major and area sources. As we reopen these rules, either to reissue them due to a court decision or to amend them as a result of a risk or technology review, we intend to add provisions that facilities submit required emissions and performance data to EPA electronically.

c) Defining the term "substantial reduction" to track progress in reducing non-cancer health impacts

The EPA air toxics program targets both cancer and non-cancer health effects. For example, the residual risk program targets, among other things, facilities with a non-cancer hazard index greater than one as a potential candidate for further evaluation and potential controls. As noted previously, directly measuring risks reductions for purposes of developing a pre-1990 baseline for the urban strategy is not feasible. As a surrogate, EPA plans to use toxicity weighted inventories to track progress in risk reductions for both cancer and non-cancer health effects. Despite the fact that we have not defined the term "substantial reduction," based on estimates from our latest available emissions inventory, emissions associated with carcinogens have been reduced by about 36 percent, while reductions from non-cancer emissions have gone down by over 50 percent from pre-1990 levels.

Also, while EPA has not issued formal definitions of terms such as "geographic hot spots" and "disproportionate impacts" as noted in the report, we continue to identify the locations of highest potential risks with tools such as NATA. These lists are frequently shared with our state, tribal and local partners to validate, and, where appropriate, take actions on reducing these risks. EPA has developed tools to compare risks across census tracts and include demographic, educational and monetary status. As directed by the Administrator, these tools will inform decision-making processes in future rulemaking efforts.

Education and Outreach

Although not the focus of the draft evaluation report, education and outreach is one of the four components of the national strategy. As such, we wanted to highlight the following accomplishments:

- EPA's Integrated Urban Air Toxics Strategy has been featured at the OAR's annual Air Toxics Training Workshops for the EPA regional staff, as well as state, tribal, and local agency staff. OAR has also held meetings with state and local agencies, including a Federal Advisory Committee Act panel (on state, local, and tribal program structure), to determine the best way to support their air toxics programs. OAR worked with environmental justice communities and others to obtain feedback on implementation.

- In coordination with the Office of Enforcement and Compliance Assurance (OECA), OAR is assisting in the development of guidance that: (1) prioritizes the area source rules to help delegated agencies and EPA regions focus their limited resources on the most significant standards to achieve emission reductions to the greatest extent possible; (2) identifies recommended approaches to ensuring compliance with individual rules; and (3) provides delegated agencies flexibility to address regionally significant issues. In addition, the guidance addresses other implementation issues such as data reporting.

- OAR continues to provide training opportunities for state, tribal, and local air agencies through webinars and webcasts on various area source rules and toxics projects, such as the chemical manufacturing and paints and allied products area source rules. In addition, OAR continues to create implementation tools and outreach materials for area source rules. OAR is currently updating classroom materials on controlling gaseous emissions, and is reviewing other topics (e.g., area source MACT standards).

Response to Recommendations

2-1 Develop and submit the required 2nd Urban Air Toxics Report to Congress by the end of FY 2010

EPA has not yet submitted the 2nd Report to Congress identified in CAA Section 112(k)(5). We have begun working on the report, and currently plan to complete it in late summer 2011. Therefore, EPA agrees with recommendation 2-1, but only insofar as it calls for the Agency to complete the Report to Congress identified in CAA Section 112(k)(5). We will prepare the report consistent with the requirements of Section 112(k)(5).

2-2 Determine how the Agency will measure progress in meeting the goals of the Strategy. If the Assistant Administrator determines that the development and maintenance of a pre-CAA baseline is not cost effective, EPA should develop and inform Congress of the Agency's alternative measures for assessing its progress in meeting the intent of the statutory goals.

EPA agrees with recommendation 2-2, insofar as the recommendation calls for EPA to determine how to measure progress in meeting the goals of the Strategy.

Conclusion and Path Forward

Recently, Administrator Jackson announced an Agency priority to reduce emissions of HAP from stationary sources and to focus on improving health and environmental quality in communities. In addressing sources of air toxics, EPA can directly effect change in communities and urban areas. In consideration of these concerns and EPA's priorities, OAR is developing a strategy for addressing HAP that will be carried out in cooperation with other EPA Offices; other federal, state and local environmental and health agencies; and other stakeholders, to reduce exposure to HAP in our communities. OAR is partnering with OECA, whose priorities for enforcement complement OAR's priorities for reducing HAP in communities and urban areas through compliance assistance and enforcement.

Other offices within EPA, other federal agencies, state, tribal and local organizations are also focused on improving health in vulnerable communities and for vulnerable sub-populations. OAR will continue to involve others as we implement this strategy, will seek partnerships wherever possible, and will continue to seek technical expertise where it will enhance our mutual efforts.

As part of the strategy under development, OAR intends to take into consideration the natural overlap of certain HAP and criteria pollutant rules and coordinate the development and implementation of major and area source HAP rules and new source performance standards where it makes sense. By coordinating MACT development for specific source categories with other rulemaking efforts, EPA can substantially reduce the cost of developing standards while providing more certainty and lower cost for industry and small businesses. At the same time, we can simplify implementation for states, tribes and local agencies, and enhance cost-effective approaches. Focusing on aspects of industrial emissions not fully addressed by previous regulatory actions, such as startup/shutdown/malfunction emissions, will also provide substantial health benefits at the local level in urban communities. Moreover, for the first time in almost a decade, OAR has shifted funds from other programs into the air toxics program to help meet some of its statutory mandates. We believe that, together, all of these actions will help address air toxics in urban areas throughout the country.

Thank you again for the opportunity to comment on the draft evaluation report. If you have any questions regarding my comments, please contact me or Steve Page, Director of OAR's Office of Air Quality Planning and Standards, at (919) 541-5616.

cc: Beth Craig, OAR
       Elizabeth Cotsworth, OAR
       Steve Page, OAR/OAQPS
       Gregory Green, OAR/OAQPS/OID
       Peter Tsirigotis, OAR/OAQPS/SPPD
       Lydia Wegman, OAR/OAQPS/HEID
       Richard Wayland, OAR/OAQPS/AQAD
       Peter South, OAR/OAQPS
       Kay Holt, OAR/OAQPS
       Michael Boucher, OAR/OAQPS
       Margo Oge, OAR/OTAQ
       Kathryn Sargeant, OAR/OTAQ
       David LaRoche OAR
       Wendy Blake, OGC
       Rick Beusse, OIG
       Jim Hatfield, OIG

OIG Evaluation of Agency Comments

The Agency's overall response states, in part, "EPA has made significant strides in reducing emissions of HAP through both its regulatory and non-regulatory actions conducted under the authority of the Clean Air Act (CAA) Section 112. Despite this progress, we agree that much remains to be done to ensure healthy, clean air for all Americans, particularly those living in urban areas where emission sources can be more concentrated and those living in communities near facilities emitting HAP." We agree that much remains to be done to ensure clean air for all Americans, particularly those living in urban areas. The remainder of the Agency's response is divided into six sections. We address each of those six sections below.

1. Response to Agency's <u>Overview of Accomplishments, Challenges, and Funding Issues</u>

The Agency comments list several of EPA's accomplishments in reducing air toxics emissions. In particular, OAR lists the issuance of numerous MACT standards, area source (GACT) standards, residual risk standards, and mobile source air toxics regulations. The Agency also noted that ambient monitoring data show decreases in ambient air toxics concentrations. However, the Agency's comments acknowledge that despite progress, more should be done. The Agency cites a 70 percent cut in funding since FY 2001 as impairing its ability to fully implement its air toxics program.

We acknowledge that EPA has completed many specific actions to implement its overall air toxics program. However, the objective of our review was to assess the Agency's tracking of its progress in meeting the urban air toxics actions mandated by the 1990 CAA Amendments and the specific goals outlined in the CAA-mandated Urban Air Toxics Strategy. As described in our report, EPA has not tracked its progress in reducing the public health risk from exposure to urban air toxics, the goal set out by CAA Section 112(k). Further, given the localized nature of air toxics concentrations, a general decrease in air toxics emissions nationwide does not necessarily mean that air toxics levels and health risks have been reduced in specific urban areas. Consequently, despite EPA's actions, the success of these actions in reducing the public health risks from exposure to air toxics in urban areas is still unknown.

2. Response to Specific Comments that CAA Actions Remain Unimplemented

The Agency's response acknowledged that certain CAA-required activities remain unimplemented. The Agency provided updates and some explanations for these delays.

As required by the 1990 CAA Amendments, EPA was to have promulgated air toxics emissions standards for all area source categories by November 15, 2000. OAR noted that the Administrator signed a proposed standard covering two area source categories in

April 2010. Our report includes the number of finalized – not proposed – rules as of January 2010, so we did not make this change to the report. In addition, OAR's comments state that three area source categories still need final standards, while our analysis shows that four categories still need standards. These four source categories are Industrial Boilers; Institutional/Commercial Boilers; Sewage Sludge Incineration; and Brick and Structural Clay Products. OAQPS told us at our exit conference that Brick and Structural Clay Products was no longer considered an area source category. If these rules are finalized by the court-ordered deadline of December 16, 2010, EPA will have satisfied the 1990 CAA Amendment requirements to promulgate air toxics emissions standards for all area source categories a little over 10 years after the original deadline.

A second key CAA action not implemented by EPA involves awarding at least 10 percent of the grant funds available under CAA Section 112 to State or local agencies to fund innovative strategies for reducing air toxics emissions from area sources. OAR commented that Congress has never appropriated grant funds to the Agency under CAA Section 112. Rather, Congress has appropriated grant funds to EPA under CAA Sections 103 and 105 to be awarded to State, local, and other air pollution control agencies to administer programs that prevent and control air pollution, and to implement national ambient air quality standards. EPA noted that it has issued annual program guidance encouraging the use of these funds to support such activities. The Agency also noted that neither Section 103 nor 105 carries a 10 percent set-aside requirement, and that EPA has used other avenues, such as the CARE initiative, to target some funds for priority air toxics needs. We revised the report to clarify that Congress has never specifically appropriated funds for CAA section 112 grants. Our report already cited EPA's CARE program in the Noteworthy Achievements section.

Nonetheless, the intent of CAA Section 112(k) has never been met. Even though Congress used CAA Sections 103 and 105 to appropriate grant funds to EPA for it to award to State and local agencies to control both air toxics and criteria pollutants, EPA could still provide 10 percent of the air toxics-related grant funds to meet the intent of CAA Section 112. However, EPA is using the manner of the Congressional appropriation as a reason it has never met the intent of the 1990 CAA Amendments that 10 percent these funds would be used for area sources emission reduction strategies. We continue to believe EPA can meet the intent of the 1990 CAA Amendments by setting aside 10 percent of the amount it allocates to air toxics activities for grants to implement innovative area source reduction strategies.

A third key CAA action that remains unimplemented is the CAA-required second report to Congress that was due in 2002. Such a report would provide Congress, State and local agencies, stakeholders, and the public transparency and accountability regarding the status of the Agency's actions to address urban air toxics. Additionally, in both its reports to Congress, EPA was to have specifically identified those urban areas that continue to experience high risks to public health posed by emissions from area sources. EPA's July 2000 first report to Congress did not do this. EPA said that the Agency will meet the requirements of CAA Section 112(k)(5) in its second report to Congress, which it stated it plans to issue in summer 2011. CAA Section 112(k)(5) requires that EPA report on the "actions taken under this subsection [CAA 112(k)] and other parts of this Act to reduce the risk to public health posed by the release of hazardous air pollutants from area sources. The reports shall also identify specific metropolitan areas that continue to experience high risks to public health as the result of emissions from area sources."

3. Response to Specific Actions Outlined in EPA's Strategy But Not Implemented (per the Draft Report)

EPA commented that its work over the past decade has further refined its thinking about air toxics and ways to reduce public exposure to air toxics. As a result, the Agency says it is in better position to reevaluate the recommendations it made in its 1999 Strategy and its September 2001 work plan. This section discusses the Agency's comments on and our evaluation of three specific actions that are outlined in its Urban Air Toxics Strategy but that it has not implemented:

- establishing a minimum risk-based air toxics program for S/L/T agencies;
- measuring and tracking progress in meeting the Strategy's goals; and
- defining the term "substantial reduction" to track progress in reducing noncancer health impacts.

First, EPA said that developing a program that sets risk-based health limits nationwide may not be the best approach to reducing risks in urban areas. The Agency cited the complexities associated with such an approach and the varying nature of air toxics problems from State to State as reasons for questioning this approach to reducing air toxics risks in urban areas. The Agency stated that it plans to reexamine this approach in conjunction with its development of the second report to Congress. Given the time lapse since the original Strategy, and the delays in tracking and addressing urban air toxics it may be prudent for EPA to reexamine the approaches it outlined in its 1999 Strategy and the associated 2001 work plan. However, EPA has had more than a decade to develop the risk-based program at the S/L/T level, as discussed in the Strategy and associated work plan, or to develop an alternative approach in its absence. EPA's response does not explain how EPA will help those State and local agencies that have laws preventing them from implementing environmental regulations stricter than EPA's regulations. We believe any revised Strategy should include firm milestones and monitoring strategies to assure that any new or revised actions or alternative approaches are implemented as expeditiously as practicable within a reasonable timeframe. Also, absent establishment of a minimum, federally required risk-based program, EPA should explain how all State and local agencies will be able to implement programs to adequately address the health risks from urban air toxics. If EPA only addresses CAA Section 112(k)(5) in its second report to Congress, as stated in its comments, the results of this reexamination would not be included in the report.

Second, with regard to measuring the Agency's progress in implementing the Strategy, EPA commented that direct measurement of both cancer and noncancer health effects and associated risks is not feasible for the purpose of establishing a baseline against which to measure progress. Instead, EPA stated that it believes other available data can be used as surrogates to measure the change in health risks to the public. The Agency stated that it believes its current air toxics measure for its annual reporting requirement (i.e., toxicity-weighted emissions inventory measures) can serve as a surrogate for measuring progress toward the CAA's goal of a 75 percent reduction in the incidence of cancer attributable to exposure from air toxics emitted from stationary sources nationwide. We acknowledge that direct measurement of cancer and noncancer health effects associated with air toxics exposure is not feasible, and that surrogate measures are needed. The use of the toxicity-weighted emissions for measuring progress toward the 75 percent reduction in cancer incidence goal is an improvement over the use of gross emissions reductions as a measure, in that it weights the reductions based on their toxicity. However, as EPA explained when it published its Integrated Urban Air Toxics Strategy in 1999, this approach lacks the dispersion and exposure modeling steps of an exposure assessment and therefore cannot provide quantitative estimates of risk. Such quantitative estimates of risk are needed to assess whether the goals of the Strategy are being met. If EPA decides to use toxicity-weighted emissions to measure progress with the 75 percent reduction in cancer goal, we note that EPA's FY2010 target is a 36 percent reduction in toxicity-weighted emissions (for cancer risk) from 1993, not a 75 percent reduction.

EPA's response also discussed the Agency's current and planned activities to gather additional air toxics measurement data and improve its current measurement efforts, such as the National Emissions Inventory and NATA. In addition to the Agency's 20 National Air Toxics Trend Sites in urban areas, EPA pointed out that it has also initiated air toxics monitoring at 65 schools, many of which are located in urban areas. Further, in 2011, EPA plans to award community-scale grants, many of which will focus on urban air toxics. These efforts follow the 53 community-scale grants EPA issued from 2004 to 2008 that were designed to, among other things, characterize the degree and extent of local air toxics problems and track progress of air toxics reduction activities. EPA also plans to improve the quality of its emissions inventory data for air toxics by addressing data quality issues through its future stationary source rules for major and area sources. As EPA reopens these rules, it intends to add provisions requiring that facilities submit emissions and performance data directly to EPA electronically. We believe these are worthwhile activities. However, EPA should explain how it will use these data to measure progress with the Strategy's goals.

Third, EPA acknowledges that it has not defined the terms "substantial reduction," "geographic hot spots," or "disproportionate impacts," which are key terms included in Goals No. 2 and No. 3 of the Strategy. Further, EPA does not state that the Agency has any plans to define them. Undefined, these terms are vague and subject to individual interpretation, and they contribute to a lack of accountability for the urban air toxics program. We continue to believe that to measure progress in achieving the Strategy's goals, these terms should be defined.

4. Education and Outreach

In this section of its response, the Agency outlined some of its activities to provide education and outreach to its air toxics program partners and stakeholders. Our report did not discuss education and outreach; therefore, we have no response to these comments.

5. Response to Recommendations

In response to Recommendation 2-1, EPA agreed to submit the second report to Congress but did not agree to address several specific items we recommended. While these items are not specifically outlined in the CAA requirements for reporting to Congress, we believe the inclusion of these items is necessary to fully inform Congress of the status of the urban air toxics program, and that it is appropriate for the Agency to do so after 20 years of implementing the 1990 CAA's urban air toxics provisions.

In response to Recommendation 2-2, the Agency agreed to determine how it will measure progress in meeting the goals of the Strategy, but did not agree to inform Congress of these plans if development of a 1990 or similar baseline is not feasible.[18] We believe informing Congress of the Agency's plan to measure urban air toxics progress without using a 1990 or similar year baseline as a starting point is necessary since the CAA Amendments specified that ". . . ambient concentrations characteristic of large urban areas should be reduced to levels substantially below those currently experienced." We revised Recommendation 2-2 by replacing the phrase "pre-CAA baseline" with "1990 or similar baseline" to clarify the intent of our recommendation.

At our exit conference the Agency said it would reassess its response to the recommendation when preparing its corrective actions plan. We are keeping both recommendations open in our tracking systems pending our receipt and analysis of the Agency 90-day corrective actions plan in response to this final report.

6. Conclusion and Path Forward

The Agency commented that the Administrator recently announced an Agency priority to reduce emissions of air toxics from stationary sources and to focus on improving health and environmental quality in communities. In light of these priorities, the Agency stated that OAR is developing a strategy to reduce exposure to air toxics in our communities that will be carried out in cooperation with other EPA offices; other federal, State, and local environmental and health agencies; and other stakeholders. OAR is partnering with the Office of Enforcement and Compliance Assurance, whose priorities for enforcement complement OAR's priorities for reducing air toxics in communities and urban areas through compliance assistance and enforcement. We acknowledge the Agency's renewed efforts to address air toxics health risks. These and other comments in the Agency's response indicate that the Agency is taking a revised and updated approach to addressing air toxics. Accordingly, we believe the Agency should formally revise its 1999 Strategy to reflect its new approach to addressing urban air toxics.

---

[18] Text originally said "if development of a pre-CAA baseline is not feasible," which we realized could be misinterpreted. During our exit meeting, OAQPS said the text was interpreted as a 1990 or similar baseline, as we had intended. We made this technical correction throughout the final report

Distribution

Office of the Administrator
Assistant Administrator for Air and Radiation
Director, Office of Regional Operations
Agency Follow-up Official (the CFO)
Agency Follow-up Coordinator
General Counsel
Associate Administrator for Congressional and Intergovernmental Relations
Associate Administrator for Public Affairs
Audit Follow-up Coordinator, Office of Air and Radiation
Acting Inspector General

www.ingramcontent.com/pod-product-compliance
Lightning Source LLC
Chambersburg PA
CBHW081758280526
45789CB00008B/2910